DINOSAUR DOODLES
FOR KIDS

CHRIS SABATINO

GIBBS SMITH
TO ENRICH AND INSPIRE HUMANKIND

Manufactured in Altona, Manitoba, Canada in
October 2012 by Friesens

First Edition
16 15 14 13 12   15 14 13 12 11 10 9 8 7 6 5 4 3

Published by
Gibbs Smith
P.O. Box 667
. Layton, Utah 84041

1.800.835.4993 orders
www.gibbs-smith.com

Designed by Renee Bond

Gibbs Smith books are printed on either
recycled, 100% post-consumer waste, FSC-
certified papers or on paper produced from
sustainable PEFC-certified forest/controlled
wood source. Learn more at www.pefc.org.

ISBN 13: 978-1-4236-3084-5

Draw yourself as a dinosaur!

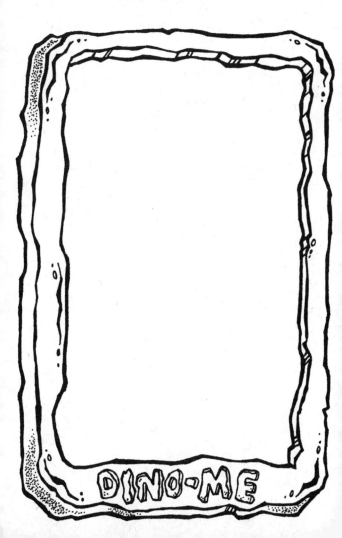

Draw the *Tyrannosaurus*'s teeth.

Draw the wings on this *Pterodactyl*.

Draw a dinosaur you'd like to take to school.

Draw the look on your teacher's face when you bring a dinosaur to class.

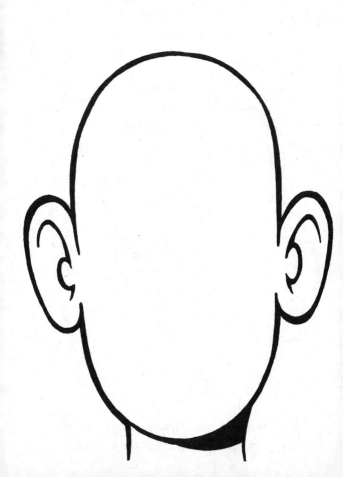

Dinosaurs have tiny brains. Draw
what's in this dinosaur's skull.

X-RAY MACHINE

Create the dinosaur's X-ray.

The *Deinonychus* is a meat eater. What's it planning on eating for lunch?

Draw the *Deinonychus* getting dessert.

A mousetrap is made to
catch a mouse. Design a trap
to capture a dinosaur.

Draw a dinosaur caught in this tar pit.

Dinosaurs and humans didn't really exist at the same time . . . but they do in this book! Draw a caveperson.

Doodle the creature this cowboy caveman is riding!

What's hatching from
this dinosaur egg?

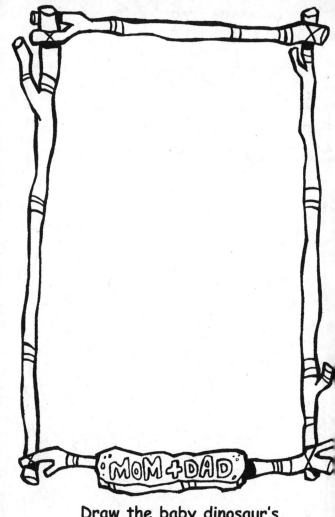

Draw the baby dinosaur's
proud parents.

Draw the creature frozen in this giant block of ice from the Ice Age.

What would this *Velociraptor* keep as a pet?

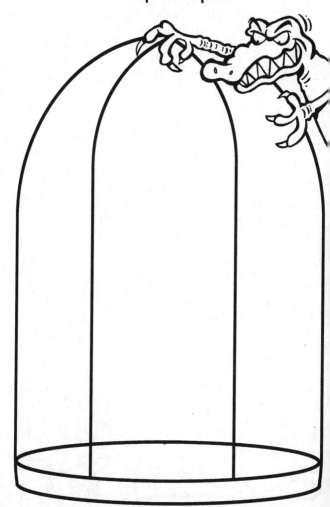

Draw the cavekid sliding down this dinosaur's back.

Draw the big dinosaur on the other side of this seesaw.

The caveman is creating a cave drawing of a dinosaur. Doodle it!

What do dinosaurs draw?

Draw the *Triceratops*'s two big horns on its forehead and one on its nose.

Finish drawing the wild tusks on this woolly mammoth.

Draw a dancing dinosaur!

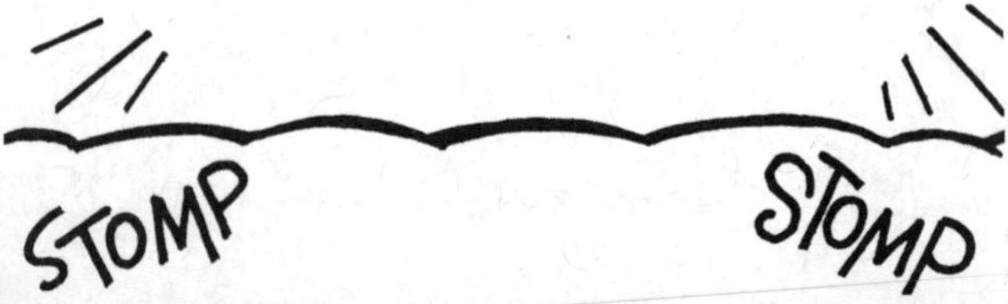

STOMP

STOMP

Create a dinosaur rock star!

I'M THE BIGGEST STONE AGE ROCKER!

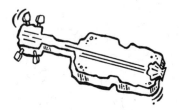

The *Elasmosaurus* swam in the ocean. Create some sea creatures for it to swim with.

Draw an *Elasmosaurus* diving into your neighbor's swimming pool!

Create a friendly dinosaur
you'd like to hang with.

Draw the scariest dinosaur you can imagine!

Draw yourself as a paleontologist (someone who searches for fossils).

Draw a cool fossil you've dug up.

A *Stegosaurus* has tall bony
plates along the ridge of
its back. Draw them.

Don't forget the four spikes
on the *Stegosaurus*'s tail!

Create a *Dog-osaurus*: half dog, half dinosaur.

Can you doodle a *Cat-osaurus*?

Prehistoric insects were huge! Create a flyswatter to swat this mega-bug.

The *Microceratus* was one of the smallest dinosaurs—about the size of a cat. What's chasing it?

Draw the space dinosaur's spaceship.

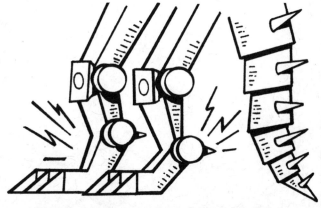

Finish drawing the robot dinosaur.

Scientists aren't sure if dinosaurs had hair or not. Give these dinosaurs some cool hairdos.

Draw the dinosaur that's attacking your town.

Design a house where you'd be safe from dinosaurs.

It's Thanksgiving and you're having
roasted dinosaur. Draw it!

What does the dinosaur want for Christmas?

A *Diplodocus* is a plant
eater. Draw lots of plants
and trees for it to eat.

Draw a *Diplodocus* invading the produce section of your supermarket.

Draw the mini-dinosaur in the science teacher's shirt pocket.

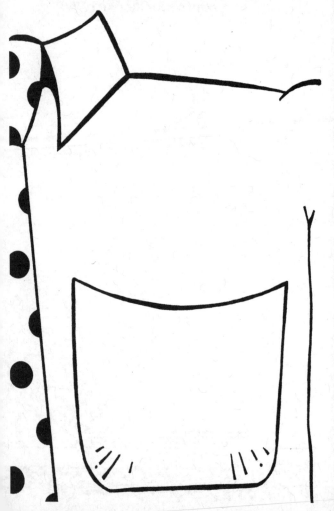

What is the giant dinosaur about to stomp on?

Doodle the king of the dinosaurs.

What is the dinosaur juggling?
Rocks? Eggs? Cavepeople?

Create Dinosaur Man, a superhero with the powers of a dinosaur.

Turn this *Triceratops* into a Stone Age police officer: a Tricera-cop!

What do they sell at the dino-store?

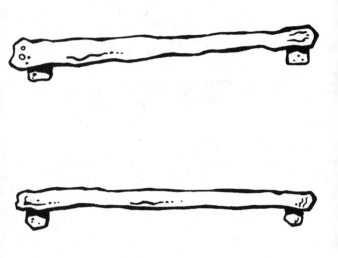

Doodle a dinosaur car made of stones and wood.

Draw your favorite dinosaur
from the movies or television.

What would a dinosaur watch on TV?

Draw a sleepy dinosaur:
a dino-snore.

Create a clown dinosaur:
a silly-saurus.

What if Noah had saved the dinosaurs?

Draw dinosaurs on his ark.

Finish drawing this dinosaur skeleton in the natural history museum.

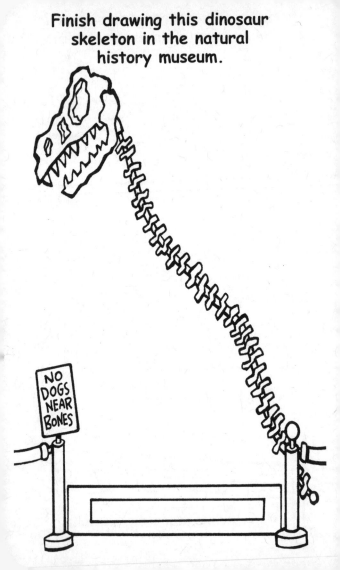

Finish this painting displayed in the museum's dinosaur exhibit.

The *Troodon* was one of the smartest dinosaurs. Create its Stone Age computer.

Draw a *Troodon* taking a science quiz.

Finish drawing the smelly *Skunk-osaurus*.

Doodle tattoos all over
this *Tattoo-osaurus.*

Draw a dinosaur popping out
of the 3-D movie screen.

What scares a dinosaur? Draw it!

Draw your teacher as a dinosaur.

What's on this dinosaur's lunchbox?

Draw what this *Triceratops*
is dreaming about.

Draw this *Pterodactyl*'s nightmare.

Draw the top part of this dinosaur.

Draw the bottom portion
of this dinosaur.

Draw a dinosaur on top of the Empire State Building.

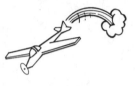

Draw the giant underwater dinosaur sneaking up on this swimmer.

Draw a skateboarding dinosaur.
(And don't forget its helmet!)

Draw the gnarly marine dinosaur this caveman is using as a surfboard.

The magician is pulling a dinosaur
out of his hat. Draw it!

**Finish drawing this
dinosaur butterfly.**

Create the inside of this Stone Age family's cave home.

Finish drawing the dinosaur angel.

Create a dinosaur devil.

Create outfits for these dinosaurs.

Draw the dinosaur these cavekids are riding to school.

Create the flying dinosaur these cavepeople are using for an airplane.

Draw two wild dinosaurs fighting.

Draw a giant stone boom box for the rapping raptor, and create some rhymes for him to rap.

Some raptors are known for
stealing other dinosaur's eggs.
Draw a raptor stealing
these Easter eggs.

Draw all the fossils under the ground.

Create a wild dinosaur that hasn't been discovered yet.

Draw a dinosaur in the dinosaur zoo.

Create a circus dinosaur.

Draw some dinosaur-shaped clouds.

Instead of a snowman, doodle a snow dinosaur (use carrots for horns and teeth).

This girl is half dinosaur. Draw her bottom dinosaur half.

Draw the top half of this
half boy/half dinosaur.

What is the *Triceratops* selling on the side of the road? Fill in the sign.

What are the dinosaurs protesting?
Fill in their picket signs.

What are the dinosaurs laughing at? Draw it.

How many dinosaurs can fit in the
back of this minivan? Draw them!

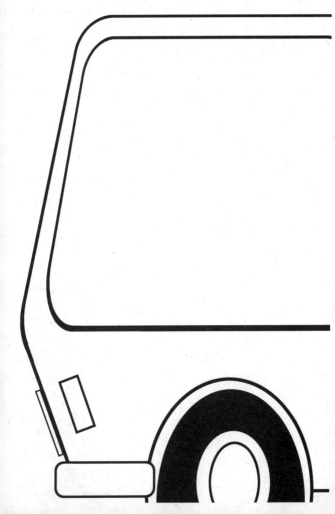

Draw the dinosaur that jumped over the moon.

If you kiss a frog, it might become a prince. Draw what happens if you kiss a dinosaur.

Instead of sheep, this girl
counts tiny dinosaurs to
fall asleep. Draw them.

Spike is obsessed with dinosaurs. Draw what's on his hat, shirt, cup, and book.

Draw what this boy's riding
on the dinosaur-go-round.

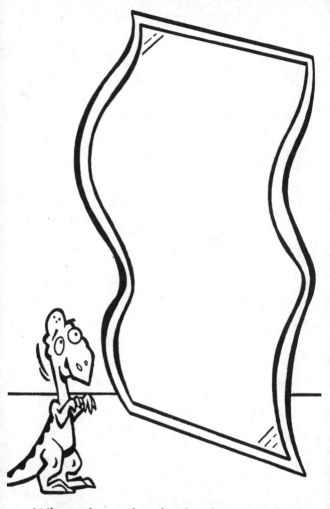

What does this little dinosaur look like in this fun-house mirror?

What are they saying?

What are they thinking?

A dinosaur opened his own store at the mall. What did he name it?

Fill the dog's shopping cart with a lot of giant dinosaur bones.

This dinosaur has chicken pox.
Draw the pockmarks on its face.

This chicken has dinosaur pox.
Draw the pockmarks on its face.

Draw this *Triceratops*'s twin.

Finish drawing this three-
headed dinosaur.

Sauroposeidon dinosaurs grew up to sixty feet tall. Draw your house next to this one.

Draw a very tall dinosaur playing basketball.

Draw the left side of this dinosaur's face.

Draw the right side of this dinosaur's face.

Draw two dinosaurs flying across the sky.

What's this *Pterodactyl* carrying in its feet?

What's pulling this dinosaur's tail?

This cavekid got caught doodling on a dinosaur. What was he drawing?

Draw the scary dinosaur this caveman caught!

Draw the photo on the front
page of this newspaper.

LOCAL NEWS

DINOSAUR DESTROYS SCHOOL!
STUDENTS SAY "COOL"!

What's the cover of this
magazine look like?

Doodle a design on this dinosaur's pajamas.

Draw some warm winter clothes on this dinosaur.

Draw the dinosaurs'
Stone Age school.

Draw a dinosaur enjoying this bubble bath.

Create a breakfast cereal a dinosaur would enjoy.

Draw the amazing time machine
this scientist invented.

Draw the prehistoric horror coming out of the time machine.

Create a dinosaur
that's half spider.

Create a creature that's half dinosaur and half porcupine.

Draw the dinosaur-shaped
cookies this boy is eating.

Draw the human-shaped cookies this dinosaur is eating.

This boy's being haunted
by the ghost of a dinosaur.
Draw the dinosaur ghost!

The evil scientist has created a dinosaur monster! What's it look like?

Draw the alien spaceship that's abducting this dinosaur.

Doodle a dinosaur of the future.

What do you get a dinosaur for its birthday?

What's coming out of this dinosaur's piñata?

This kid is dressed as a dinosaur for Halloween. Create the kid's costume.

Draw a picture of a dinosaur outlaw on this wanted poster.

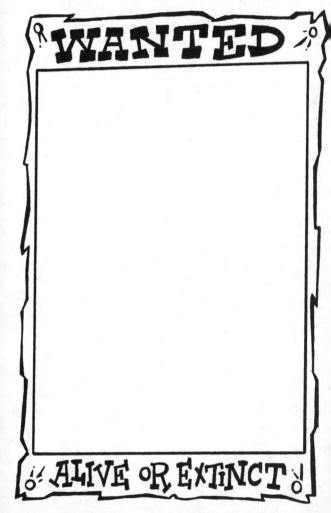

What are they saying?

What is the parachutist thinking?

Create a dinosaur vampire.

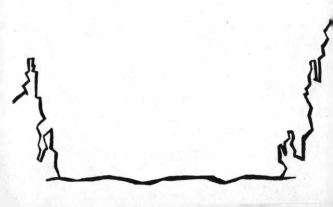

The potion is turning nice
Dr. Jekyll into scary Mr. Dinosaur!
Draw Mr. Dinosaur.

Draw the dinosaur under your bed.

There's a dinosaur skeleton
in your closet. Draw it!

Who's riding this bronco-saurus?

What is Tyrannosaurus Tex lassoing?

Draw some dinosaurs playing ice hockey.

Create a dinosaur opera singer.

Draw a crown and gown for this Jurassic beauty contest winner.

What is the cavegirl lifting?

Create the caveboy's prehistoric bike.

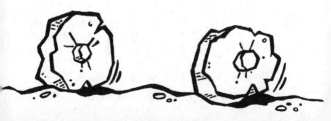

Draw the dinosaur hunter
trapped in the tree.

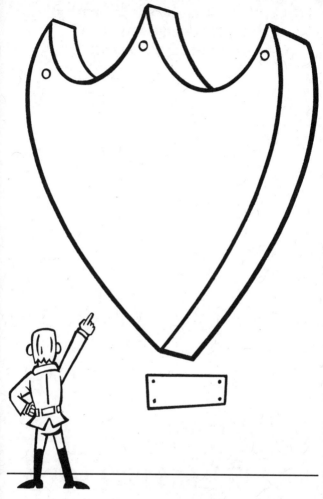

Draw the dinosaur head mounted
on the dinosaur hunter's wall.

On their way to Oz, Dorothy
and her friends meet an
enchanted dinosaur.

Wake up, Goldirocks! The Papa, Mama, and Baby Dinosaur are home.

Draw a sweater on this woolly mammoth.

The cavewoman made the dinosaur a very cool hat. Draw it!

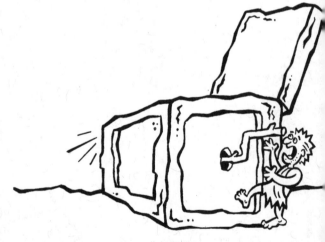

Draw what's popping out of
the dinosaur-in-the-box.

Draw the rest of this spinning *Triceratops* top.

The cavepeople are using a
dinosaur as a bridge across
the river. Draw it.

Draw the bridge's toll collector, too!

Draw the giant dinosaur balloon in the parade.

How many balloons will it take to lift this dinosaur? See how many you can draw!

What does the caveman
see in the cave?

What does the dinosaur see in the sky?

Draw what's in the big box being delivered to the museum.

Draw the human exhibit in the dinosaur museum.

Dinosaurs in the playground. Who you gonna call? Dino-busters! Draw the dinosaurs the Dino-busters are trying to control.

What's the caveman hitting with his club?

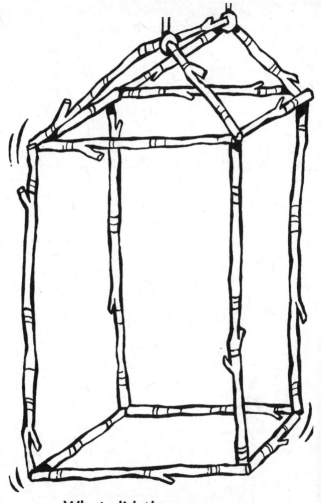

What did the cavewoman
capture in the cage?

Draw a giant dinosaur looking in the school window.

Draw the tiny dinosaur this girl carries in her backpack.

How many dinosaurs does it take to change a lightbulb? Draw them.

Look! It's a *Tic-tac-toe-osaurus*!

Draw yourself talking to
this chatty dinosaur.

Someone you know has been
swallowed by a dinosaur. Draw
them in the dinosaur's tummy.

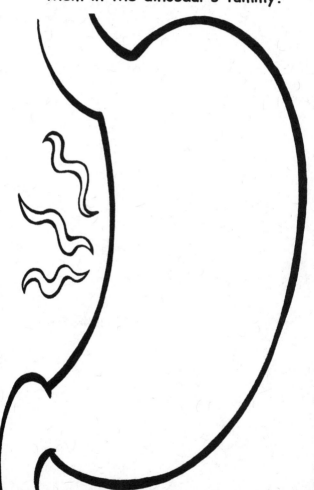

Draw the king of the cavepeople riding on the back of this dinosaur.

Draw the prehistoric view outside the caveperson's window.

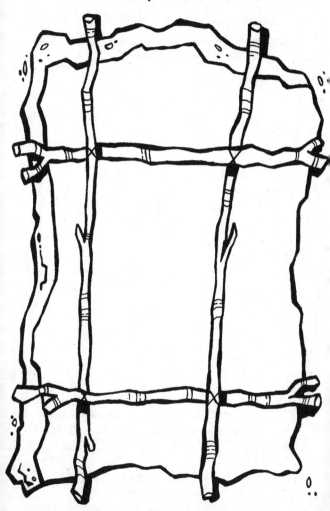

What movie is playing at the Dinosaur Drive-in?

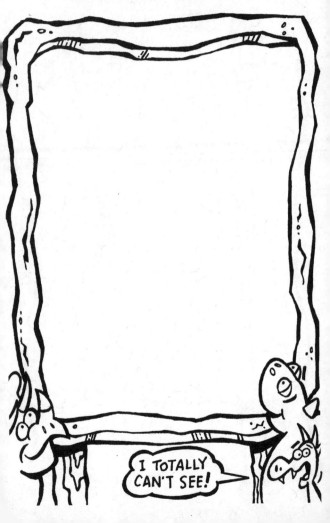

What do dinosaurs eat at the movies?

Draw more dinosaurs on the dance floor at the dinosaur disco.

SOMEDAY
DINOSAURS
AND DISCOS
WILL BE
DEAD!

Create a Stone Age monster made of rocks!

Doodle a dinosaur-eating plant.

The paleontologists looking for fossils found a giant dinosaur footprint. Draw it.

Draw one of the paleontologists
caught in quicksand.

Oh, no! There's a dinosaur playing on the other soccer team!

A dinosaur is playing George Washington in your school play. Draw it.

QUIT HOGGING THE STAGE, DUDE!

Draw an epic battle between dinosaurs and space invaders!

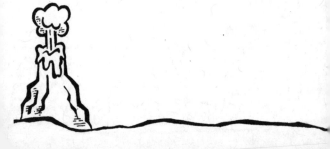

Forget the pail of water! Jack and Jill found a dinosaur in the well!

London Bridge is falling down . . .
because there's a dinosaur on it!

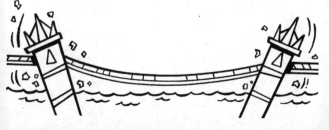

What is the saber-toothed tiger attacking?

Draw a saber-toothed kitten playing with this giant ball of yarn.

Fill this nest with dinosaur eggs.

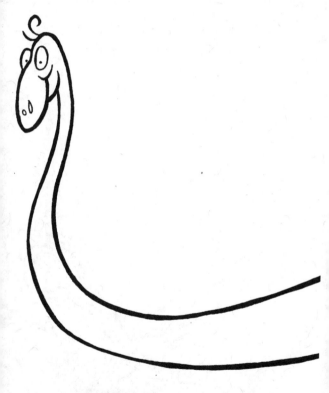

Draw this dinosaur's babies
sitting on her neck.

Draw a dinosaur popping out of this Stone Age cuckoo clock.

Draw the sundial watch on the caveperson's wrist.

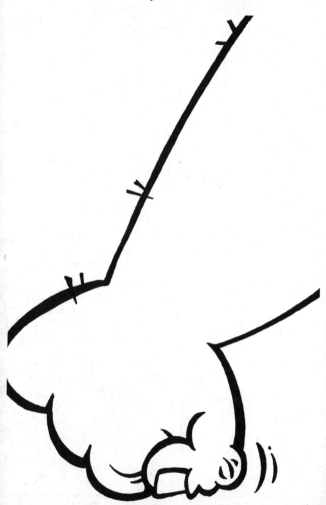

Fossils eventually turn
into fuel after millions of
years in the ground. Draw
a dinosaur pumping gas.

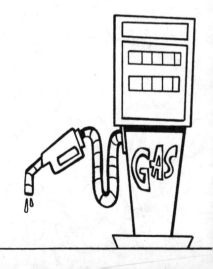

You planted some dinosaur seeds.
Draw what grew from them!

Most things we know about dinosaurs we learned from fossils. What's this fossil saying?

A dinosaur is calling your cell phone. Draw its picture I.D.

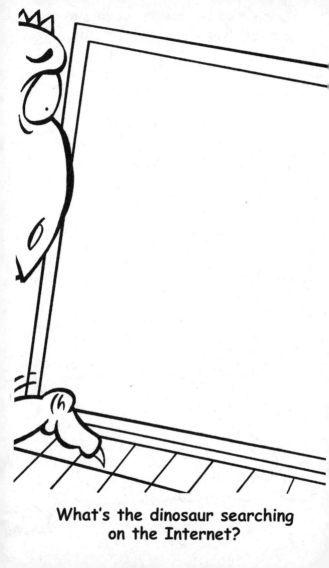

What's the dinosaur searching
on the Internet?

Draw two dinosaurs having a tug-of-war over the tar pit.

What's perched on the pirate dinosaur's shoulder?

Draw a dinosaur walking the plank.

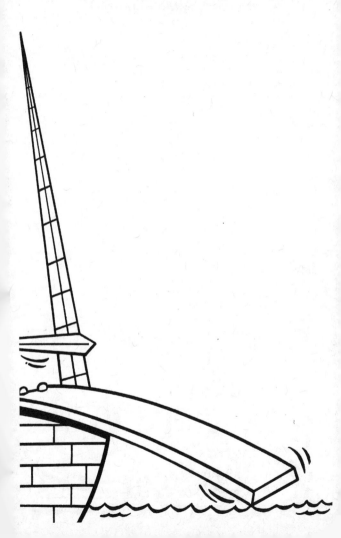

Doodle what's being shot out
of the dinosaur's cannon.

And what's the dinosaur shooting at?

Someone put a note on the dinosaur's back. What does it say?

Create a *Pig-osaurus*.

What is the *Triceratops* busting through?

Who is this dinosaur butting heads with?

Make this dinosaur into
a businessperson.

Change this dinosaur into a witch.

A *Comic-osaurus* is a dinosaur that loves comic books. Draw one enjoying this awesome comic book!

Finish drawing this comic book cover.

Finish drawing this dinosaur comic.

IT LOOKS LIKE A GIANT SNAKE!
OR A GIANT... TAIL!
IT IS A GIANT TAIL! ON THE BIGGEST, SCARIEST, CREATURE EVER!
RUN! RUN AWAY!

The scouts run into a
prehistoric horror! Draw it.

There's a dinosaur outside
the tent! Draw its shadow.

Draw all the riders on the dinosaur train.

What's in the window at The Dinosaur Pet Shop?

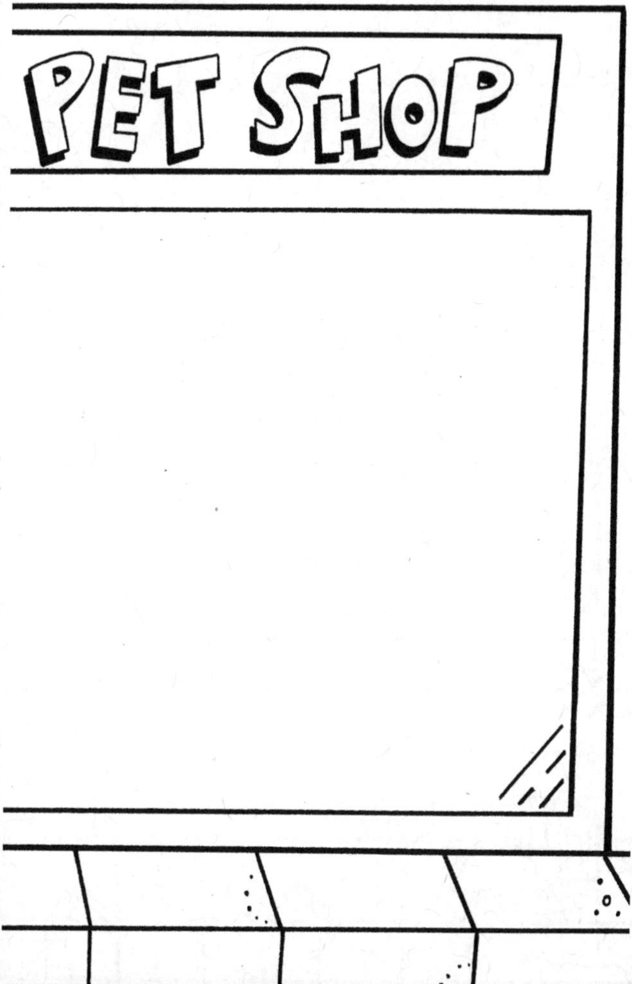
PET SHOP

The pet dinosaur in your backyard is making your neighbors nervous. Draw it.

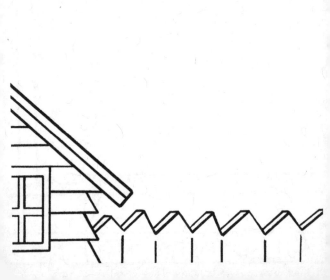

Design a dinosaur house—like a doghouse—to keep your pet in.

We don't know if dinosaurs actually had ears—but if they did, what might they look like? Here are some possibilities to draw.

MOUSE EARS

CLOWN EARS

ELF EARS

ELEPHANT EARS

RABBIT EARS

MARTIAN ANTENNAS

Draw what's on the front page
of this Stone Age newspaper.

What's the caveman selling at this yard sale?

Draw what's living on
Dinosaur Island.

A giant keeps a collection of
dinosaurs in its cave. Fill this bottle
with dinosaurs the giant's caught.

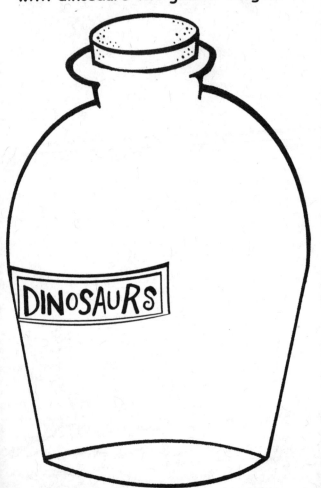

Who's walking up this dinosaur's back?

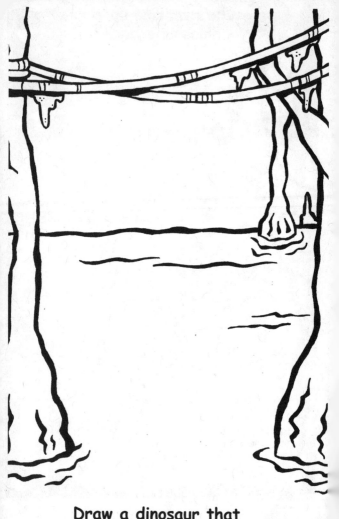

Draw a dinosaur that
lives in this swamp.

Doodle a dinosaur that
lives underground.

Draw your family as cavepeople.

Draw the dinosaur running for president on this campaign poster.

THE BEST CANDIDATE FOR THE FUTURE IS ONE FROM THE PAST!

It's the singing Dino Diva!
Draw her backup dancers.

What are they thinking?

What are this bird and dinosaur arguing about?

Some believe a large meteor
hit the earth and wiped
out the dinosaurs. Draw a
meteor about to crash.

Others think erupting volcanoes
destroyed the dinosaurs.
Draw smoke and lava coming
out of the volcanoes.

Draw what *you* think happened
to cause the extinction
of the dinosaurs.

Some scientists now believe that dinosaurs never actually became extinct—they just evolved into birds!

Draw some present-day "dinosaurs"
hanging out on this tree limb.

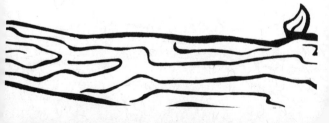

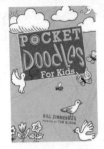